Master Guide to Making Money on YouTube

Jagdish Pareek

DEDICATION

Dedicated to my loving wife, Gayatri and my daughters
Kalpana and Priyanka.

CONTENTS

ACKNOWLEDGMENTS

I would like to express my sincere gratitude to my family and friends who have supported me in this project. I especially want to thank Gayatri (my wife) for never ending support and being patient all the time when I was busy with my adventures on my personal computer
.

I would also like to thank my daughters, Kalpana and Priyanka who have encouraged me to carry out my passion and provided invaluable feedback and guidance

Thanks to Gaurav and Pawan for their valuable help in editing the book. Finally, I would like to thank my readers for their interest in my work.

CHAPTER ONE

Monetize your channel with YouTube Ads: Enable monetization on your channel to earn money from the ads that play before, during, or after your videos

One of the most common and accessible ways to make money on YouTube is by monetizing your channel with YouTube Ads. When you enable monetization, ads will be displayed before, during, or after your videos, and you earn a portion of the revenue generated from these advertisements. This revenue is based on factors such as ad impressions, viewer engagement, and the ad format itself.

To get started, you'll need to meet the eligibility requirements set by YouTube. These requirements include having at least 1,000 subscribers on your channel and accumulating 4,000 watch hours within the past 12 months. Once you meet these thresholds, you can apply for the YouTube Partner Program, which grants you access to various monetization features.

Enabling monetization on your channel is a straightforward process. Go to your YouTube Studio dashboard, navigate to the "Monetization" tab, and follow the prompts to set up an AdSense account. AdSense is Google's advertising platform that manages the ad placements on your videos and handles the payment process. Linking your AdSense account to your YouTube channel will allow you to receive earnings from your ad revenue.

It's important to note that not all videos are eligible for monetization. YouTube has strict policies in place to ensure that the content is suitable for advertisers and the wider audience. It's crucial to familiarize yourself with these guidelines and create videos that comply with them to maintain monetization eligibility.

Once your channel is monetized, ads will start appearing on your videos. The types of ads you may encounter include skippable ads, non-skippable ads, display ads, overlay ads, and sponsored cards. These ads provide opportunities for you to generate revenue based on the ad impressions and viewer interactions.

The amount of money you can earn through YouTube Ads varies and is influenced by several factors. The ad formats and placements, the number of ad impressions, the viewer engagement with the ads, and the demographics of your audience all play a role in determining your earnings. Additionally, the ad rates can fluctuate based on the time of year, advertiser demand, and the niche of your content.

To maximize your ad revenue, it's essential to focus on creating high-quality content that attracts and engages your target audience. The more views and watch time your videos accumulate, the higher the potential for ad impressions and earnings. Consistency in uploading new content and optimizing your videos for search visibility can also contribute to increased viewership and ad revenue.

While YouTube Ads can be a significant source of income, it's important to note that it might take time to build a substantial revenue stream. Initially, the earnings may be modest, but as your channel grows and attracts more viewers, the potential for higher ad revenue increases. It's crucial to remain dedicated, continue improving your content, and explore additional monetization avenues to supplement your earnings.

In conclusion, enabling monetization on your YouTube channel and utilizing YouTube Ads is a popular and accessible way to make money on the platform. By meeting the eligibility requirements and creating content that complies with YouTube's policies, you can start earning revenue from the ads that play before, during, or after your videos. While the earnings may vary, focusing on producing high-quality content and growing your channel can increase your ad revenue over time. So, if you're ready to turn your passion into a profitable venture, monetizing your channel with YouTube Ads is a valuable step towards achieving your financial goals on YouTube.

CHAPTER TWO

Explore Sponsored Content: Collaborate with brands and create sponsored videos or product placements to earn money for promoting their products or services.

In the vast world of YouTube, sponsored content has become a popular avenue for content creators to monetize their channels. By collaborating with brands and incorporating sponsored videos or product placements into their content, YouTubers have the opportunity to earn money while promoting products or services that align with their niche and audience.

Sponsored content refers to videos where creators work in partnership with brands to showcase their offerings to their viewers. These collaborations can take various forms, such as dedicated product reviews, tutorials, hauls, or endorsements within the context of the content creator's videos. It's crucial to ensure that the sponsored content feels authentic and seamlessly integrates with the creator's style and audience expectations.

To explore sponsored content opportunities, content creators can start by identifying brands that align with their niche and have products or services relevant to their audience. Conducting thorough research on the brand's values, target audience, and previous collaborations will help ensure a good fit. Many brands have dedicated influencer marketing departments or work with influencer marketing agencies, making it easier for creators to initiate contact and establish collaborations.

When negotiating sponsored content deals, it's essential for content creators to consider factors such as the scope of work, compensation, disclosure requirements, and the creative freedom they retain. Clear communication with the brand is crucial to ensure that both parties understand and agree on the expectations and deliverables. It's also important to comply with legal guidelines and disclose sponsored content to viewers transparently, following the Advertising Standards Authority (ASA) guidelines in the UK.

When creating sponsored videos, content creators need to maintain their authenticity and connection with their audience. They should strive to provide honest and unbiased opinions about the products or services they promote. Building trust with their viewers is paramount, and promoting products that align with their audience's interests and needs can strengthen that trust. Content creators should only collaborate with brands and promote products that they genuinely believe in to maintain their credibility and integrity.

The compensation for sponsored content collaborations can vary depending on factors such as the content creator's reach, engagement, and negotiation skills, as well as the brand's marketing budget and goals. Payments can take the form of a flat fee, a commission-based structure, free products or services, or a combination thereof. Content creators need to evaluate the value they provide and negotiate fair compensation that reflects their influence and the effort required to create the sponsored content.

While sponsored content can be a lucrative way to monetize a YouTube channel, content creators should be mindful of striking a balance between sponsored and non-sponsored content. Overloading their channel with sponsored videos may alienate their audience and diminish their authenticity. It's crucial to find a balance that benefits both the content creator and their viewers, ensuring that the sponsored content enhances the overall viewer experience and aligns with their interests.

Successful sponsored content collaborations not only benefit content creators financially but can also open doors to further opportunities. Positive relationships with brands can lead to long-term partnerships, repeat collaborations, or invitations to exclusive events or product launches. These collaborations can enhance a content creator's credibility and visibility within their niche, attracting more brand partnerships in the future.

In conclusion, exploring sponsored content is a viable pathway to monetizing a YouTube channel. Collaborating with brands and creating sponsored videos or product placements allows content creators to earn money while promoting products or services that resonate with their audience. By maintaining authenticity, transparency, and integrity throughout the sponsored content process, content creators can build trust with their viewers and establish fruitful, long-term partnerships with brands. As always, striking a balance between sponsored and non-sponsored content is crucial to ensure a positive viewer experience and continued success in the world of sponsored content on YouTube.

CHAPTER THREE

Join the YouTube Partner Program: Meet the eligibility requirements and join the YouTube Partner Program to gain access to additional monetization features like channel memberships and Super Chat.

The YouTube Partner Program (YPP) is an exclusive program that allows content creators to monetize their YouTube channels and access additional features to enhance their earning potential and audience engagement. By meeting specific eligibility requirements, content creators can unlock a range of monetization tools and interact with their viewers in new and exciting ways.

To join the YouTube Partner Program, content creators must meet certain criteria set by YouTube. The primary requirements include having at least 1,000 subscribers on their channel and accumulating 4,000 watch hours within the past 12 months. These thresholds are designed to ensure that creators have an engaged and active audience before they can monetize their content.

Once the eligibility requirements are met, content creators can apply for the YouTube Partner Program through their YouTube Studio dashboard. YouTube will review the application to ensure that the channel complies with its policies and community guidelines. If the application is approved, the content creator becomes a YouTube Partner and gains access to a variety of monetization features.

One of the key benefits of joining the YouTube Partner Program is the ability to earn money through advertisements displayed on the channel's videos. Content creators can enable monetization on their channels, and YouTube will place ads before, during, or after their videos. The revenue generated from these ads is shared with the content creator, providing an opportunity to earn income based on factors such as ad impressions and viewer engagement.

In addition to ad revenue, content creators in the YouTube Partner Program can unlock other monetization features such as channel memberships and Super Chat. Channel memberships allow content creators to offer exclusive perks and benefits to their most loyal fans. Subscribers can pay a monthly fee to become members and gain access to special badges, emojis, and exclusive content. This feature not only generates additional revenue but also fosters a sense of community and strengthens the connection between content creators and their audiences.

Super Chat is another powerful tool available to YouTube Partners. It enables viewers to pay to have their messages highlighted during a live stream or premiere. By purchasing Super Chats, viewers can grab the content creator's attention, have their messages displayed prominently in the chat, and show their support. This feature not only allows content creators to engage with their audience in real-time but also provides an additional revenue stream during live streams or premieres.

Joining the YouTube Partner Program opens the door to various opportunities for content creators to grow their channels and expand their revenue streams. As YouTube continues to evolve, the platform frequently introduces new monetization features and updates to enhance the creator experience. By being a part of the YouTube Partner Program, content creators gain access to these innovations and can adapt their strategies to leverage the latest tools.

While joining the YouTube Partner Program presents exciting possibilities, content creators must remember to adhere to YouTube's policies and community guidelines. It's crucial to continue creating quality content that aligns with the platform's guidelines and resonates with its audience. Maintaining a strong presence and engaging with their viewers through regular uploads, community posts, and live interactions can contribute to building a loyal and supportive fanbase.

In conclusion, joining the YouTube Partner Program offers content creators a gateway to enhanced monetization opportunities and additional features that foster audience engagement. By meeting the eligibility requirements and becoming a YouTube Partner, content creators can monetize their channels through advertisements and access tools like channel memberships and Super Chat. However, it is important to continue producing high-quality content and nurturing the relationship with the audience to ensure long-term success on YouTube. By embracing the YouTube Partner Program and its accompanying benefits, content creators can thrive in the dynamic and ever-growing YouTube community.

CHAPTER FOUR

Utilize Affiliate Marketing: Promote products or services through affiliate links in your video descriptions and earn a commission for every sale or sign-up generated through your referral.

Affiliate marketing is a powerful monetization strategy that allows content creators on YouTube to promote products or services and earn a commission for driving sales or sign-ups through their affiliate links. By leveraging their influence and audience trust, content creators can tap into a vast array of affiliate programs and earn passive income while providing value to their viewers.

To begin utilizing affiliate marketing, content creators need to sign up for affiliate programs relevant to their niche. Many brands and online retailers offer affiliate programs, where they provide unique tracking links or discount codes that content creators can incorporate into their video descriptions. When viewers click on these affiliate links and make a purchase or sign up for the promoted service, the content creator earns a commission, often based on a percentage of the sale or a fixed amount per sign-up.

When selecting affiliate programs, content creators need to choose products or services that align with their niche and resonate with their audience. Promoting items that are genuinely valuable and relevant to their viewers' interests enhances trust and credibility. It's crucial to maintain transparency and disclose any affiliate relationships to viewers to ensure ethical and responsible marketing practices.

To effectively incorporate affiliate marketing into their videos, content creators should focus on creating engaging, informative, and entertaining content. Simply bombarding viewers with promotional messages is unlikely to yield positive results. Instead, content creators should strive to educate their audience about the benefits and features of the promoted products or services, offering genuine insights and personal experiences.

Creating dedicated product reviews, and tutorials, or showcasing the products in action can be highly effective in conveying the value and usefulness of the items being promoted. By highlighting how the products or services can solve a problem or enhance the viewers' lives, content creators can encourage their audience to make a purchase or sign up through their affiliate links.

The success of affiliate marketing lies in the content creator's ability to build trust with their audience. Regularly producing high-quality and reliable content establishes credibility and fosters a loyal fanbase. By consistently recommending products or services that genuinely provide value, content creators can strengthen the trust their audience places in them, leading to increased conversions and commissions.

Additionally, content creators can enhance the effectiveness of their affiliate marketing efforts by optimizing their video descriptions and incorporating clear calls to action. Including the affiliate links prominently in the video descriptions, along with compelling and persuasive text, encourages viewers to click and explore the promoted products or services. It's important to strike a balance between being informative and persuasive, avoiding excessive sales pitches that may alienate the audience.

Tracking the performance of affiliate marketing efforts is crucial to evaluate the success of different promotions and optimize future strategies. Most affiliate programs provide analytics and reporting tools that allow content creators to monitor the number of clicks, conversions, and commissions earned. This data can be used to identify top-performing products, understand audience preferences, and refine the affiliate marketing approach.

In conclusion, affiliate marketing presents a lucrative opportunity for content creators on YouTube to monetize their channels by promoting products or services and earning commissions for driving sales or sign-ups. By selecting affiliate programs that align with their niche, creating engaging content, and building trust with their audience, content creators can effectively leverage affiliate marketing to generate passive income.

CHAPTER FIVE

Create and Sell Merchandise: Develop your lines of branded merchandise, such as t-shirts, hats, or mugs, and sell them to your loyal audience.

Creating and selling merchandise is an exciting and profitable way for content creators on YouTube to engage with their audience while generating additional income. By developing a line of branded merchandise, such as t-shirts, hats, or mugs, content creators can showcase their unique style and offer their loyal fans a tangible way to support their channel.

To get started with creating and selling merchandise, content creators should first consider their brand identity and the preferences of their audience. Understanding the demographics, interests, and preferences of their viewers is crucial in developing merchandise that will resonate with their fanbase. This includes considering factors like the design, colors, and styles that align with the content creator's image and the expectations of their audience.

Once the design concept is established, content creators can explore various options for producing their merchandise. There are numerous print-on-demand services and e-commerce platforms available that handle the production, printing, and shipping processes, allowing content creators to focus on the creative aspects of their merchandise. These services typically require minimal upfront investment and offer the flexibility to experiment with different designs and products.

Designing merchandise that reflects the content creator's brand and aesthetic is essential in creating a strong connection with its audience. The merchandise should be visually appealing, high-quality, and showcase the content creator's unique style. Incorporating elements from their channel, such as catchphrases, logos, or inside jokes, can create a sense of exclusivity and identity for their loyal fans.

In addition to apparel items like t-shirts, hoodies, and hats, content creators can also consider other merchandise options, such as accessories, stationery, or lifestyle products, depending on their niche and audience preferences. It's important to diversify the range of merchandise to cater to different tastes and provide options for fans with varying interests.

Promoting and marketing the merchandise is a crucial step in driving sales and generating interest from the audience. Content creators can leverage their YouTube channel, social media platforms, and other online communities to showcase their merchandise and encourage their viewers to make a purchase. Engaging with their audience through dedicated merchandise launch announcements, unboxing videos, or wearing the merchandise themselves in their videos can create excitement and encourage their fans to support them.

Building a strong sense of community and exclusivity around the merchandise can also be effective in driving sales. Content creators can consider offering limited edition or seasonal merchandise, creating a sense of urgency and desirability. Additionally, organizing giveaways, discounts, or bundling options can incentivize viewers to make a purchase and help spread the word about the merchandise to a wider audience.

Managing inventory and fulfillment is a crucial aspect of running a successful merchandise business. Partnering with reliable print-on-demand services or e-commerce platforms ensures that orders are fulfilled efficiently and customer service is maintained. Regularly monitoring inventory levels, addressing customer inquiries, and ensuring timely shipping and delivery contribute to a positive buying experience for the audience.

Another important consideration for content creators is the financial aspect of selling merchandise. Determining the pricing strategy requires careful consideration of production costs, shipping fees, platform fees, and desired profit margins. Conducting market research, analyzing competitors' pricing, and understanding the perceived value of the merchandise to the audience can help in setting a price that is attractive to buyers while ensuring a reasonable profit.

In conclusion, creating and selling merchandise offers content creators on YouTube an exciting opportunity to connect with their audience and generate additional income. By developing a line of branded merchandise that resonates with their fans, content creators can showcase their unique style and provide a tangible way for their audience to show their support. With the availability of print-on-demand services and e-commerce platforms, the process of producing and selling merchandise has become more accessible than ever. By effectively promoting and marketing the merchandise, managing inventory and fulfillment, and setting appropriate pricing, content creators can build a thriving merchandise business that enhances their brand, strengthens their connection with their audience, and contributes to their overall revenue streams.

CHAPTER SIX

Offer Online Courses or Coaching: Share your expertise and knowledge by creating online courses or offering personalized coaching sessions to your viewers.

One of the most valuable assets a content creator possesses is expertise and knowledge in a specific niche. By leveraging this expertise, content creators on YouTube have the opportunity to monetize their skills by offering online courses or personalized coaching sessions to their viewers. This not only allows content creators to generate additional income but also provides a platform for them to share their insights and help others in their respective fields.

Creating an online course is an effective way for content creators to package their knowledge and deliver it to a broader audience. Online courses can be designed as a comprehensive curriculum or focused on specific topics within the content creator's niche. Through a series of video lessons, downloadable resources, quizzes, and assignments, content creators can provide valuable educational content to their viewers.

When developing an online course, content creators should identify the specific pain points or needs of their audience and design the course to address those challenges. Breaking down complex concepts into digestible modules, incorporating real-life examples, and providing actionable advice can enhance the learning experience and ensure the course's value. It's important to maintain a balance between providing valuable content and engaging the audience to encourage their active participation.

To deliver online courses, content creators can utilize various e-learning platforms or create their membership sites. E-learning platforms offer user-friendly interfaces, built-in payment systems, and a wide reach to potential students. These platforms handle the technical aspects of hosting the course, managing student enrollments, and providing analytics to track the course's performance. Alternatively, content creators can opt to create their membership sites, giving them full control over the course structure, pricing, and student interactions.

In addition to online courses, content creators can offer personalized coaching sessions to their viewers. Coaching provides an opportunity for content creators to work closely with their audience, offering one-on-one guidance and support tailored to their specific needs. Whether it's career coaching, fitness training, or personal development, content creators can leverage their expertise and experience to help individuals achieve their goals.

Personalized coaching sessions can be conducted through video calls, email exchanges, or online chat platforms. Content creators can offer different coaching packages based on the duration and level of support required. This allows them to cater to a range of budgets and provide flexibility to their audience in choosing the coaching option that best suits their needs.

When offering online courses or coaching services, content creators need to establish their credibility and demonstrate their expertise in their respective fields. Building a strong reputation and gaining the trust of their audience is crucial for attracting students or clients. Content creators can achieve this by consistently delivering high-quality content on their YouTube channel, showcasing their achievements and success stories, and sharing testimonials from satisfied students or clients.

To effectively promote online courses or coaching services, content creators can utilize their YouTube channel, social media platforms, and email newsletters. By highlighting the benefits and value of the courses or coaching, content creators can pique the interest of their viewers and encourage them to enroll. Offering limited-time discounts, early bird registrations, or bonuses can create a sense of urgency and entice potential students or clients to take action.

Managing the logistics of online courses and coaching services requires careful planning and organization. Content creators should establish clear communication channels with their students or clients, provide timely feedback and support, and ensure that the learning or coaching experience is smooth and seamless. Regularly collecting feedback and making improvements based on student or client suggestions can contribute to the ongoing success and reputation of the courses or coaching services.

In conclusion, offering online courses or personalized coaching sessions provides content creators on YouTube with a valuable opportunity to monetize their expertise and knowledge. By creating well-designed online courses and delivering valuable educational content, content creators can empower their viewers to learn and grow in their respective fields. Additionally, offering personalized coaching allows content creators to work closely with individuals, providing tailored guidance and support to help them achieve their goals. By establishing credibility, effectively promoting the courses or coaching services, and ensuring a seamless learning or coaching experience, content creators can build a thriving educational business while making a positive impact on the lives of their audience.

CHAPTER SEVEN

Seek Brand Sponsorships: Reach out to companies directly or join influencer marketing platforms to secure brand sponsorships and create dedicated content for their products or services.

Brand sponsorships offer content creators on YouTube a fantastic opportunity to collaborate with companies and monetize their channels while creating dedicated content for their viewers. By partnering with brands, content creators can not only earn a substantial income but also gain access to exciting products, exclusive events, and unique experiences.

To seek brand sponsorships, content creators can adopt two main approaches: reaching out to companies directly or joining influencer marketing platforms. Direct outreach involves identifying brands that align with the content creator's niche and target audience and then contacting them to propose a collaboration. This method requires research, as content creators should carefully select brands that resonate with their channel's theme and values.

When reaching out to companies, content creators should focus on demonstrating their unique selling points, highlighting their audience demographics and engagement metrics, and showcasing their previous successful collaborations or branded content. Creating a compelling pitch that clearly outlines the benefits of partnering with the content creator can significantly increase the chances of securing sponsorships.

In addition to direct outreach, content creators can leverage influencer marketing platforms. These platforms act as intermediaries, connecting content creators with brands looking for influencer partnerships. By joining these platforms, content creators gain access to a pool of brands actively seeking collaborations, making the process more streamlined and efficient. Influencer marketing platforms provide an opportunity for content creators to showcase their profiles, metrics, and portfolio to attract brands interested in their niche.

When selecting brand sponsorships, content creators should prioritize aligning with brands that genuinely resonate with their audience and complement their content. It's essential to maintain authenticity and avoid partnering with brands solely for financial gain. By selecting brands that share common values and interests with their channel, content creators can ensure that their sponsored content feels organic and adds value to their viewers' experience.

Creating dedicated content for brand sponsorships requires a delicate balance between promotional messaging and providing value to the audience. Content creators should strive to integrate the brand seamlessly into their videos, ensuring that it aligns with their content style and engages their viewers. Simply delivering scripted product placements may come across as inauthentic, potentially alienating the audience. Instead, content creators should focus on showcasing the benefits and features of the sponsored products or services in a genuine and relatable manner.

To maximize the impact of brand sponsorships, content creators can consider developing unique and creative concepts that highlight the brand's offerings. This can involve incorporating the product into a storyline, conducting an in-depth review, or hosting a giveaway or contest for viewers to participate in. By engaging their audience and encouraging interaction, content creators can create a memorable experience that resonates with their viewers and increases the effectiveness of the sponsored content.

Transparency is key when creating branded content. Content creators must disclose their partnership with the brand to maintain trust and ethical practices. This can be done through clear and conspicuous disclosures within the video or in the video description. Openly sharing that the content is sponsored ensures transparency and builds credibility with the audience.

When negotiating brand sponsorships, content creators should consider factors such as compensation, deliverables, and exclusivity. Compensation can vary depending on factors such as the content creator's reach, engagement metrics, and the scope of the collaboration. Deliverables should be clearly outlined, specifying the number and type of videos or promotional materials required, as well as the expected timeline for delivery. Exclusivity clauses should also be discussed, determining whether the content creator is allowed to collaborate with competing brands during a specific period.

Managing brand sponsorships requires effective communication and professionalism. Content creators should maintain a good relationship with the brand representatives, promptly responding to their inquiries, and delivering the agreed-upon deliverables on time. Nurturing positive partnerships can lead to long-term collaborations and potential future sponsorships.

In conclusion, seeking brand sponsorships provides content creators on YouTube with a lucrative opportunity to monetize their channel while creating dedicated content for their viewers. Whether through direct outreach or influencer marketing platforms, content creators can collaborate with brands that align with their niche and audience. By creating authentic and valuable sponsored content, maintaining transparency, and nurturing positive partnerships, content creators can successfully integrate brand sponsorships into their channel, enhancing their income and offering unique experiences to their audience.

CHAPTER EIGHT

Crowdfunding and Fan Donations: Engage with your viewers by setting up crowdfunding campaigns or enabling fan donations through platforms like Patreon or PayPal.

Crowdfunding and fan donations have emerged as powerful avenues for content creators on YouTube to connect with their audience on a deeper level while receiving financial support. By setting up crowdfunding campaigns or enabling fan donations through platforms like Patreon or PayPal, content creators can foster a sense of community, reward their most dedicated fans, and gain the necessary financial backing to sustain and enhance their content.

Crowdfunding campaigns provide a platform for content creators to seek financial support directly from their viewers. Platforms like Kickstarter, Indiegogo, or GoFundMe allow content creators to present their projects or content ideas to a wider audience and request financial contributions. These campaigns can range from funding a new series, purchasing equipment, or financing a special project that aligns with the content creator's vision.

To create an effective crowdfunding campaign, content creators should communicate their goals, aspirations, and the impact the funds will have on their channel. It's essential to provide a compelling narrative that resonates with the audience and highlights the value they will receive by contributing to the campaign. Offering exclusive rewards, such as early access to content, merchandise, or personalized shoutouts, can incentivize viewers to contribute at different donation levels.

Fan donation platforms like Patreon have gained popularity among content creators on YouTube. Patreon allows content creators to set up membership tiers and offer exclusive perks and content to their supporters. By enabling fans to make recurring monthly donations, content creators can establish a stable source of income and cultivate a closer relationship with their most loyal audience members.

When setting up Patreon tiers, content creators should carefully consider the value they provide to their supporters at each level. This can include access to behind-the-scenes content, exclusive live streams, bonus videos, or direct interaction through private messaging or community forums. It's crucial to strike a balance between offering enticing perks and maintaining sustainability, ensuring that the workload associated with fulfilling the perks is manageable.

Integrating fan donations through platforms like PayPal is another way to engage with viewers and provide them with the option to contribute financially. PayPal offers simple and secure payment processing, allowing content creators to accept one-time donations from their audience.

This approach provides flexibility for viewers who may not want to commit to recurring contributions but still wish to support the content creator.

To encourage fan donations, content creators can mention and promote their crowdfunding campaigns or fan donation options within their videos, video descriptions, or social media posts. Expressing gratitude and regularly acknowledging the support received from fans can help foster a sense of appreciation and encourage others to contribute. Content creators can also highlight how fan donations directly contribute to the improvement and sustainability of their content, making viewers feel like they are an integral part of the creative process.

Managing and rewarding supporters through crowdfunding and fan donations requires effective communication and organization. Regularly updating backers or donors on the progress of the campaign or providing exclusive content to supporters ensures that they feel connected and valued. Content creators should also maintain transparency by sharing how the funds are being utilized and the impact it has on their channel's growth.

Content creators need to be mindful of any legal or tax obligations when receiving funds through crowdfunding or fan donations. Understanding the regulations in their jurisdiction and consulting with professionals, if necessary, can help content creators navigate any legal complexities associated with receiving financial contributions.

In conclusion, crowdfunding and fan donations present content creators on YouTube with an opportunity to engage with their viewers on a deeper level while receiving financial support. By setting up crowdfunding campaigns or enabling fan donations through platforms like Patreon or PayPal, content creators can foster a sense of community, reward their most dedicated fans, and secure the necessary funds to sustain and enhance their content. By offering exclusive rewards, maintaining transparency, and expressing gratitude, content creators can create a mutually beneficial relationship with their audience, allowing them to continue creating quality content and connecting with their viewers.

CHAPTER NINE

YouTube Channel Memberships: Offer exclusive perks, behind-the-scenes content, or early access to videos in exchange for a monthly membership fee from your loyal fans.

YouTube Channel Memberships provide an excellent opportunity for content creators on YouTube to engage with their most dedicated fans and generate a recurring income stream. By offering exclusive perks, behind-the-scenes content, or early access to videos, content creators can cultivate a sense of community and reward their loyal supporters for their ongoing support.

YouTube Channel Memberships allow content creators to create different membership tiers, each offering a unique set of benefits to subscribers. These benefits can include access to exclusive videos, live streams, community posts, badges or emojis to use in comments, priority in receiving responses to their queries, or even merchandise discounts. By providing a range of perks, content creators can cater to different levels of fan dedication and ensure that there is a value associated with each membership tier.

To effectively implement YouTube Channel Memberships, content creators should carefully consider the perks they offer at each membership level. The perks should be enticing enough to motivate viewers to become members while also being sustainable for the content creator to deliver consistently. It's important to strike a balance between providing valuable exclusive content and managing the workload associated with creating and delivering those perks.

Creating exclusive behind-the-scenes content can be an effective way to engage members and provide them with a glimpse into the content creator's creative process. This can include bloopers, Q&A sessions, vlogs, or behind-the-scenes footage that showcases the content creator's daily life or the production process of their videos. Offering this exclusive content allows members to feel connected to the content creator on a deeper level and provides a sense of exclusivity.

Early access to videos is another perk that can entice viewers to become members. Content creators can offer their members the opportunity to watch their videos before they are released to the general public. This can create a sense of excitement and exclusivity among members, as they get to experience the content before anyone else. It also serves as a way to reward their loyalty and make them feel valued.

Promoting YouTube Channel Memberships requires effective communication and marketing strategies. Content creators can promote their membership program through their videos, video descriptions, community posts, or social media channels. Clearly explaining the benefits of becoming a member and showcasing the exclusive content or perks available can encourage viewers to join. Offering limited-time promotions or discounts during the initial launch of the membership program can also create a sense of urgency and drive more sign-ups.

Engaging with members is crucial for building a strong community and fostering a sense of belonging. Content creators should actively interact with their members by responding to their comments, addressing their questions or concerns, and considering their feedback. Creating a dedicated community section or forum where members can connect and the content creator can further enhance the sense of community and provide a space for members to interact and support one another.

Managing YouTube Channel Memberships involves regular communication and consistent delivery of perks. Content creators should set clear expectations with their members, outlining the frequency and type of exclusive content they will receive. Consistency is key to maintaining member satisfaction and retention. Regularly updating members on upcoming content, addressing their feedback, and continuously evaluating and refining the perks offered can contribute to the long-term success of the membership program.

Content creators should also be mindful of the financial aspects of YouTube Channel Memberships. YouTube takes a percentage of the membership fees as a platform fee, and content creators should consider this when pricing their membership tiers. They should also be aware of any tax obligations associated with receiving income through the membership program and consult with professionals if needed.

In conclusion, YouTube Channel Memberships offer

content creators on YouTube a valuable opportunity to engage with their most dedicated fans and generate a recurring income stream. By offering exclusive perks, behind-the-scenes content, or early access to videos, content creators can create a sense of community, reward their loyal supporters, and foster a deeper connection with their audience. Effective promotion, consistent delivery of perks, and active engagement with members are essential for building a successful membership program that benefits both the content creator and their loyal fans.

CHAPTER TEN

Explore Product Reviews: Review products related to your niche and earn money through sponsored reviews or by including affiliate links in your video descriptions.

Product reviews have become a popular form of content on YouTube, offering content creators an opportunity to share their insights and recommendations with their audience. By exploring product reviews, content creators can not only provide valuable information to their viewers but also monetize their channel through sponsored reviews and affiliate marketing.

Reviewing products related to your niche allows content creators to establish themselves as trusted authorities in their respective fields. Whether it's technology, beauty, fashion, gaming, or any other niche, offering honest and detailed reviews can attract viewers who are seeking reliable information and guidance before making purchasing decisions. By delivering comprehensive and unbiased reviews, content creators can build credibility and trust with their audience, increasing the likelihood of viewers relying on their recommendations.

Sponsored reviews provide content creators with an avenue to earn money by partnering with brands. Companies may approach content creators directly or through influencer marketing platforms to request reviews of their products. These collaborations typically involve receiving free products or compensation in exchange for creating a dedicated review video. When conducting sponsored reviews, content creators must maintain transparency and disclose the sponsorship to their audience. Openly communicating the sponsored nature of the review ensures ethical practices and builds trust with viewers.

When creating sponsored reviews, content creators should strive to maintain their authenticity and impartiality. It is important to provide an unbiased assessment of the product, highlighting both its strengths and weaknesses. By delivering honest reviews, content creators can preserve their credibility and help viewers make informed decisions. Genuine feedback resonates with audiences and strengthens the bond between content creators and their viewers.

Affiliate marketing is another avenue for content creators to monetize product reviews. By including affiliate links in their video descriptions or using affiliate marketing platforms like Amazon Associates, content creators can earn a commission for every sale or sign-up generated through their referral. When viewers click on the affiliate link and make a purchase, the content creator receives a percentage of the revenue.

To effectively leverage affiliate marketing, content creators should choose products that align with their niche and are of genuine interest to their audience.

Recommending products that they have personally used and believe in enhances the trust between content creators and their viewers. Providing a clear and compelling call-to-action, encouraging viewers to use the affiliate links, and explaining the benefits of the recommended products can increase the likelihood of generating affiliate revenue.

Striking a balance between providing valuable content and incorporating affiliate links is essential. Content creators should focus on delivering informative and engaging reviews that provide viewers with insights into the product's features, functionality, and overall value. Integrating affiliate links organically within the video descriptions or mentioning them during the review allows for a seamless user experience and avoids coming across as overly promotional.

When embarking on product reviews and affiliate marketing, content creators should comply with relevant regulations and guidelines. Familiarizing themselves with advertising standards and disclosure requirements ensures transparency and ethical practices. Content creators should disclose their affiliation with the brands or the use of affiliate links to maintain trust and integrity with their audience.

Effectively promoting product reviews involves optimizing video titles, descriptions, and tags to increase visibility and attract relevant viewers. Researching popular keywords and incorporating them strategically within the video metadata can help content creators reach a wider audience. Sharing product reviews on social media platforms, engaging with viewers' comments and feedback, and encouraging viewers to share the content can also enhance the reach and impact of the reviews.

In conclusion, exploring product reviews provides

content creators on YouTube with an opportunity to deliver valuable information to their audience while monetizing their channel. Sponsored reviews allow content creators to collaborate with brands and earn money, while affiliate marketing enables them to generate revenue through product referrals. By providing honest and detailed reviews, maintaining transparency, and focusing on delivering valuable content, content creators can establish trust with their audience and create a sustainable source of income through product reviews.

CHAPTER ELEVEN

Create and Sell Digital Products: Develop digital products such as e-books, online guides, or presets, and sell them to your audience.

Creating and selling digital products has become a popular avenue for content creators on YouTube to diversify their income streams and provide additional value to their audience. By developing e-books, online guides, presets, or other digital resources, content creators can leverage their expertise and offer unique products that resonate with their viewers.

Digital products offer a range of benefits for both content creators and their audiences. They are easily accessible, cost-effective, and can be instantly delivered to customers worldwide. Content creators have the freedom to choose the format and content of their digital products, allowing them to showcase their knowledge and skills in a structured and comprehensive manner. For viewers, digital products provide a convenient way to access specialized information, tutorials, or resources created by content creators they trust and admire.

E-books are a popular digital product that content creators can develop and sell to their audience. Whether it's a guide on a specific topic, a recipe collection, a fitness program, or a self-help book, e-books provide an opportunity to package valuable content in a visually appealing and easily consumable format. Content creators can leverage their expertise and unique perspectives to create e-books that cater to the needs and interests of their audience. The content can be presented in a combination of text, images, and even videos, providing a comprehensive learning experience.

Online guides are another type of digital product that content creators can create and sell. These guides can cover a wide range of topics, such as travel itineraries, photography techniques, online marketing strategies, or personal development tips. Online guides offer a structured approach to learning and provide step-by-step instructions or actionable advice to help viewers achieve their goals. Content creators can create in-depth guides that draw on their own experiences, research, and expertise, making them valuable resources for their audience.

Presets are digital tools commonly used in photography or video editing. They allow content creators to create a specific look or aesthetic and apply it to their images or videos with just a few clicks. By developing and selling presets content creators can offer their audience the opportunity to achieve a similar visual style in their content. Presets can be customized and tailored to different editing software or specific genres, providing a versatile tool for aspiring photographers or videographers.

When creating and selling digital products, content

creators should consider the interests and needs of their audience. Conducting market research, engaging with viewers through comments or surveys, and understanding the challenges or desires of their audience can help content creators identify the most relevant and in-demand digital products to develop. By aligning the content of their digital products with the interests and preferences of their audience, content creators can maximize their sales potential.

Effectively marketing and promoting digital products is essential to their success. Content creators can leverage their YouTube channel and social media platforms to generate awareness and interest in their digital products. Creating teaser videos, offering sneak peeks, or sharing testimonials from satisfied customers can create anticipation and encourage viewers to make a purchase. Providing clear and compelling calls to action, such as limited-time discounts or bonuses, can also help drive sales and create a sense of urgency.

Content creators should also invest time and effort in creating visually appealing and professional-looking product pages or landing pages. Communicate the value and benefits of the digital product, showcase sample content or screenshots, and provide an easy and secure purchasing process.

Engaging with customer inquiries, addressing feedback or concerns promptly, and maintaining a positive reputation is crucial for building trust and ensuring customer satisfaction.

In conclusion, creating and selling digital products offers content creators on YouTube an opportunity to diversify their income streams and provide additional value to their audience. Whether through e-books, online guides presets, or other digital resources, content creators can leverage their expertise and knowledge to develop unique products that resonate with their viewers. By understanding the interests and needs of their audience, effectively marketing and promoting their digital products, and delivering high-quality content, content creators can generate revenue while enriching the lives of their audience.

CHAPTER TWELVE

Become a YouTube Partner Manager: Apply to become a YouTube Partner Manager and help other creators optimize their channels in exchange for a percentage of their earnings.

Becoming a YouTube Partner Manager is an exciting opportunity for experienced content creators to share their knowledge and expertise while generating additional income. As a Partner Managers, individuals can assist other creators in optimizing their channels, increasing their visibility, and ultimately boosting their earnings on YouTube. This role allows content creators to leverage their skills and insights to help others succeed in the dynamic world of online content creation.

The primary responsibility of a YouTube Partner Manager is to provide guidance and support to content creators in maximizing their channel's potential. This involves offering advice on various aspects of channel optimization, such as content strategy, audience engagement, search engine optimization (SEO), video production techniques, and monetization strategies. Partner Managers use their experience and expertise to help creators identify areas for improvement and implement effective strategies to enhance their channel's performance.

To become a YouTube Partner Manager, individuals typically need a proven track record of success on YouTube, with a deep understanding of the platform's algorithms, policies, and best practices. YouTube often looks for individuals who have a substantial subscriber base, consistent viewership, and a demonstrated ability to engage and retain audiences. Content creators who have effectively monetized their channels and achieved significant earnings are particularly well-suited for this role.

The application process for becoming a YouTube Partner Manager may vary, but it generally involves applying, providing evidence of past success on YouTube, and undergoing a selection process. YouTube evaluates applicants based on their expertise, communication skills, and their ability to assist and mentor other creators effectively. Successful candidates are often those who can demonstrate a genuine passion for helping others succeed and a strong understanding of the YouTube ecosystem.

Once selected, YouTube Partner Managers enter into partnerships with other content creators, offering their guidance and expertise in exchange for a percentage of the creators' earnings. The specific terms of the partnership may vary and should be negotiated between the Partner Manager and the content creator. It is common for the Partner Manager to receive a percentage of the revenue generated through monetization, sponsorships, brand deals, or other income streams associated with the channel.

As a YouTube Partner Manager, effective

communication and relationship-building skills are essential. Partner Managers must establish a strong rapport with the creators they work with, understanding their goals, aspirations, and challenges. They should be able to provide constructive feedback, actionable insights, and ongoing support to help creators continuously improve their content and channel performance. By building a trusting and collaborative relationship, Partner Managers can create an environment conducive to growth and success.

Partner Managers should stay up-to-date with the latest trends, algorithm changes, and industry developments to provide creators with relevant and timely guidance. This involves continuously learning and adapting to the evolving landscape of YouTube and the online content creation industry. By keeping their knowledge and skills current, Partner Managers can offer valuable insights and strategies that align with the ever-changing dynamics of the platform.

In addition to their role as advisors, YouTube Partner Managers can also serve as connectors and facilitators within the creator community. They can facilitate collaborations between creators, connect them with industry professionals, or help them navigate the various resources and opportunities available on YouTube. By fostering a sense of community and collaboration, Partner Managers contribute to the overall growth and success of the creator ecosystem.

In conclusion, becoming a YouTube Partner Manager offers experienced content creators a unique opportunity to share their knowledge, assist other creators, and earn additional income. By leveraging their expertise, communication skills, and understanding of the YouTube platform, Partner Managers can guide and support creators in optimizing their channels and increasing their earnings. This role requires a deep understanding of YouTube's algorithms and best practices, effective communication and relationship-building skills, and a genuine passion for helping others succeed. As the online content creation industry continues to evolve, YouTube Partner Managers play a crucial role in shaping the success of creators and the overall ecosystem of YouTube.

CHAPTER THIRTEEN

Provide Video Editing or Graphic Design Services: Utilize your editing skills to offer video editing or graphic design services to other YouTubers or businesses.

In the fast-paced world of YouTube, content creators are constantly seeking ways to improve the quality and visual appeal of their videos. This presents a lucrative opportunity for skilled individuals who possess video editing or graphic design expertise. By offering video editing or graphic design services, content creators can not only monetize their skills but also contribute to the success of other YouTubers or businesses.

Video editing services involve refining raw footage into polished, engaging, and professional-looking videos. Skilled video editors can enhance visual elements, adjust audio levels, add special effects, transitions, and graphics, and ensure a seamless flow of content. They play a crucial role in shaping the overall tone, storytelling, and impact of a video. Content creators who possess strong editing skills can leverage their expertise to offer their services to other YouTubers who may lack the time, technical knowledge, or resources to edit their videos themselves.

Graphic design services, on the other hand, focus on creating visually appealing and compelling visuals, such as thumbnails, channel banners, logos, or custom graphics for videos. Eye-catching visuals are essential for capturing viewers' attention and enticing them to click on a video. Skilled graphic designers can create visually striking assets that align with a creator's brand identity and effectively communicate the essence of their content. By providing graphic design services, content creators can help other YouTubers or businesses elevate their visual presence and attract a larger audience.

To offer video editing or graphic design services, content creators should showcase their skills and portfolio through a dedicated website or online platform. Creating a professional online presence allows potential clients to review their work, assess their style, and determine if their skills align with their needs. Content creators can include sample videos they have edited or graphic design work they have created, highlighting their creativity, technical proficiency, and attention to detail.

Building a strong reputation and client base is crucial for success in the video editing or graphic design service industry. Content creators can start by offering their services to friends, fellow YouTubers, or local businesses to gain experience and gather testimonials. Positive feedback and recommendations can help establish credibility and attract more clients. It's also beneficial to actively engage with the YouTube community, participate in relevant forums or groups, and showcase their expertise through informative blog posts, tutorials, or demonstrations.

When pricing their video editing or graphic design services, content creators should consider factors such as their skill level, the complexity of the project, and the time required to complete the work. Conducting market research and understanding industry standards can provide insights into competitive pricing. Content creators can offer different pricing packages based on the specific services provided, such as basic editing, advanced effects, or additional revisions. It's essential to be transparent about pricing and communicate the value that clients can expect to receive.

Maintaining effective communication with clients is crucial throughout the editing or design process. Content creators should establish clear expectations, discuss project requirements, and gather feedback from clients to ensure that their vision is translated into the final product. Timely delivery of high-quality work, responsiveness to client inquiries, and a collaborative approach can foster a positive client experience and result in repeat business or referrals.

Continuously updating skills and staying abreast of industry trends is essential for content creators offering video editing or graphic design services. Technology and editing techniques evolve rapidly, and content creators must adapt to stay competitive. Investing in professional software, attending workshops or online courses, and engaging in peer-to-peer learning can help sharpen skills and expand capabilities.

In conclusion, offering video editing or graphic design services presents a valuable opportunity for content creators to monetize their skills while supporting other YouTubers or businesses. By leveraging their expertise, creativity, and technical proficiency, content creators can enhance the quality and visual appeal of videos, contributing to the success of their clients. Building a strong online presence, establishing a positive reputation, and maintaining effective communication is key to attracting clients and ensuring client satisfaction. As the demand for high-quality content continues to rise, the prospects for video editing and graphic design services remain promising.

CHAPTER FOURTEEN

Live Streaming and Super Chat: Engage with your audience through live streaming and encourage them to use Super Chat to make donations or have their messages highlighted during the stream.

Live streaming has revolutionized the way content creators interact with their audience, offering a real-time and immersive experience that fosters engagement and connection. By embracing live-streaming on platforms like YouTube, content creators can not only build a loyal community but also monetize their live content through features like Super Chat.

Live streaming enables content creators to broadcast their videos in real-time, allowing viewers to tune in, interact, and participate in the experience as it unfolds. Whether it's a Q&A session, a gaming session, a tutorial, or a live event, live streaming creates a dynamic and interactive environment that fosters direct communication between content creators and their audience. It provides an opportunity for viewers to ask questions, offer feedback, share their thoughts, and engage with the content creator on a more personal level.

One of the monetization features available during live streams is Super Chat. Super Chat allows viewers to make donations to content creators during the live stream. When viewers make a Super Chat donation, their message is highlighted in the live chat, ensuring that their contribution stands out and catches the attention of the content creator and other viewers. This creates a sense of appreciation and recognition for the donor and encourages others to participate in the live chat and support the content creator.

Content creators can benefit from Super Chat in multiple ways. Firstly, it provides a direct and immediate source of income during live streams. Viewers who appreciate the content, value the interaction, or simply want to show their support can make monetary donations through Super Chat. These donations can range from small contributions to more significant amounts, depending on the viewer's generosity and appreciation for the content creator's work. Secondly, Super Chat allows content creators to better connect with their audience and strengthen the sense of community. By highlighting Super Chat messages, content creators can directly respond to these messages, acknowledge the donors, and engage in meaningful conversations during the live stream. This interaction not only deepens the relationship between the content creator and their audience but also encourages more viewers to participate and contribute to the live chat.

To make the most of live streaming and Super Chat, content creators should consider several strategies. Firstly, they should schedule and promote their live streams in advance, generating anticipation and ensuring a larger audience turnout. By notifying their subscribers and social media followers about the upcoming live stream, content creators can increase the likelihood of viewers tuning in and participating in the Super Chat feature.

During the live stream, content creators should actively engage with the audience, responding to Super Chat messages, answering questions, and acknowledging donors. This level of interaction demonstrates appreciation and creates a positive and inclusive atmosphere. Content creators can also establish specific themes or topics for their live streams, encouraging viewers to participate in discussions and providing valuable insights or entertainment that incentivizes Super Chat contributions.

Content creators need to set clear guidelines and expectations for Super Chat usage. They should communicate the purpose of Super Chat and how the donations will be utilized. Whether the donations will be used to support the channel, fund future projects, or contribute to a charitable cause, transparency fosters trust and encourages viewers to contribute to Super Chat with confidence.

Content creators should also explore additional ways to incentivize Super Chat participation. They can offer exclusive perks or rewards to donors, such as shout-outs, access to exclusive content, or early previews of upcoming videos. By providing tangible benefits to Super Chat contributors, content creators can enhance the value proposition and encourage ongoing support from their audience.

In conclusion, live streaming and the Super Chat feature offer content creators an exciting opportunity to engage with their audience in real-time and monetize their live content. By embracing live streaming, content creators can foster a sense of community, provide interactive experiences, and directly communicate with their audience. Super Chat adds a monetization element to live streams, allowing viewers to make donations and have their messages highlighted during the stream. Through effective promotion, active engagement, and transparent communication, content creators can leverage live streaming and Super Chat to enhance their connection with viewers and generate income from their live content.

CHAPTER FIFTEEN

YouTube Premium Revenue: Earn a share of the revenue generated by YouTube Premium subscribers who watch your videos.

YouTube Premium is a subscription-based service offered by YouTube that provides an enhanced viewing experience for users. Subscribers enjoy several benefits, including ad-free viewing, offline playback, and access to YouTube Originals. As a content creator, you have the opportunity to earn a share of the revenue generated by YouTube Premium subscribers who watch your videos.

YouTube Premium offers an alternative revenue stream for content creators beyond traditional advertising. While ad revenue is primarily generated through ads displayed before, during, or after videos, YouTube Premium revenue provides an additional avenue for earning income. When YouTube Premium subscribers watch your videos, you receive a portion of the subscription fees they pay for the premium service.

To be eligible for YouTube Premium revenue, you need to meet certain criteria. Firstly, you must be a member of the YouTube Partner Program and have an active AdSense account linked to your YouTube channel. This ensures that you are set up to monetize your content through various channels, including YouTube Premium. Additionally, your content must meet YouTube's guidelines and policies to ensure suitability for the premium viewing experience.

Once you meet the eligibility requirements, your videos become available to YouTube Premium subscribers. When these subscribers watch your content, YouTube allocates a portion of their subscription fees to you as part of the YouTube Premium revenue pool. The amount you earn is determined by factors such as the watch time of your videos by premium subscribers and the overall engagement with your content.

To maximize your earnings from YouTube Premium revenue, it's crucial to focus on creating high-quality content that appeals to a wide audience. Engaging videos that captivate viewers and encourage them to watch for longer durations can significantly increase your watch time, ultimately leading to a higher share of the YouTube Premium revenue pool. Consistency, authenticity, and providing value to your viewers are key to building a loyal subscriber base.

Promoting your channel and videos through various marketing channels can also help attract more YouTube Premium subscribers. Encourage your audience to subscribe to your channel and consider subscribing to YouTube Premium for an enhanced viewing experience. By educating your viewers about the benefits of YouTube Premium and how it supports content creators, you can increase the likelihood of earning revenue from this source.

It is important to note that YouTube Premium revenue is separate from the revenue generated through traditional advertising. It provides an additional stream of income that can contribute to your overall earnings as a content creator. Diversifying your revenue streams is essential for long-term sustainability and financial success on the platform.

Monitoring your YouTube Analytics is crucial for understanding the performance of your videos and tracking the revenue generated through YouTube Premium. The analytics dashboard provides valuable insights into the watch time of your videos, the demographics of your viewers, and the revenue generated from various sources, including YouTube Premium. This data allows you to make informed decisions, optimize your content strategy, and identify growth opportunities.

YouTube Premium revenue serves as an incentive for content creators to continue producing high-quality videos and engaging their audience. By offering premium viewers an ad-free experience and exclusive access to your content, you can attract and retain YouTube Premium subscribers who contribute to your revenue stream. Engaging with your audience, encouraging subscriptions, and creating a community around your channel can foster loyalty and support from your viewers.

In conclusion, YouTube Premium revenue offers content creators an additional source of income by earning a share of the revenue generated by YouTube Premium subscribers who watch their videos. By meeting the eligibility requirements, creating compelling content, and promoting YouTube Premium to your audience, you can maximize your earnings from this revenue stream. Monitoring your analytics and adapting your content strategy based on viewer preferences and engagement can further optimize your YouTube Premium revenue potential.

Embracing YouTube Premium as a revenue source allows you to diversify your income and build a sustainable career as a content creator on YouTube.

CHAPTER SIXTEEN

License your Content: Explore opportunities to license your videos or footage to media outlets, production companies, or stock footage platforms.

As a content creator, your videos possess unique value and potential beyond the YouTube platform. Licensing your content provides an exciting opportunity to monetize your videos by granting permission to other entities to use your footage for various purposes, such as television broadcasts, documentaries, advertisements, or online publications.

Licensing your content involves entering into agreements with interested parties who wish to utilize your videos or footage. These parties can include media outlets, production companies, advertising agencies, or even stock footage platforms. By licensing your content, you allow them to use your videos in exchange for a licensing fee or royalty payments.

There are several benefits to licensing your content. Firstly, it offers a new revenue stream separate from advertising or direct viewer support. By licensing your videos, you tap into a broader market and reach a wider audience. This can result in significant financial gains, especially if your content is in high demand or aligns with popular trends and topics. Secondly, licensing can provide exposure and recognition for your work. When your videos are used by reputable media outlets or production companies, it not only generates income but also increases your visibility as a content creator. Your videos may be seen by a larger audience, leading to increased brand recognition and potential collaboration opportunities in the future.

To license your content effectively, it's essential to protect your intellectual property and understand your rights as a content creator. Consider copyrighting your videos or obtaining necessary licenses for any copyrighted materials, such as music or artwork, that appear in your videos. This ensures that you have the legal authority to grant licenses to third parties and safeguards your work from unauthorized use.

To begin licensing your content, you can actively reach out to potential buyers or utilize online platforms that specialize in connecting content creators with buyers. Media outlets and production companies are always on the lookout for compelling and relevant footage to enhance their projects, so approaching them directly with a well-crafted pitch can yield positive results. Alternatively, you can explore stock footage platforms where you can upload and license your videos to a wide range of buyers. These platforms provide a convenient marketplace for content creators to showcase their work and connect with buyers seeking specific types of footage. By utilizing stock footage platforms, you can tap into a global network of potential buyers and maximize the exposure and licensing opportunities for your videos.

When negotiating licensing agreements, it's crucial to consider factors such as the duration of the license, the territories in which the footage will be used, and the scope of usage (e.g., television, online, or both). Clearly define the terms and conditions of the license, including the licensing fee or royalty structure, to ensure that both parties are in agreement.

Additionally, it's important to retain ownership of your content and carefully review any contracts or agreements presented to you. Seek legal advice if necessary to ensure that your rights as a content creator are protected and that you maintain control over how your videos are used. Regularly assess the market demand for your content and adapt your licensing strategy accordingly. Stay informed about industry trends, emerging topics, and current events that may increase the demand for specific types of footage. By keeping a pulse on the market, you can position yourself to capitalize on licensing opportunities and optimize your revenue potential.

In conclusion, licensing your content opens up exciting possibilities for monetizing your videos beyond the YouTube platform. By granting permission to media outlets, production companies, or stock footage platforms to use your videos, you can generate additional income and gain exposure for your work. Take steps to protect your intellectual property, explore potential buyers, and negotiate licensing agreements that align with your goals as a content creator. Embrace the opportunity to expand your reach and profitability by licensing your valuable content.

CHAPTER SEVENTEEN

Offer Video Editing Tutorials: Share your video editing techniques and create tutorials to help aspiring creators improve their editing skills.

Video editing plays a vital role in creating compelling and professional-looking content. As a skilled content creator, you have the opportunity to share your expertise and help aspiring creators enhance their editing skills through informative and engaging video editing tutorials.

Creating video editing tutorials not only provides value to your audience but also opens up a new avenue for monetization. By sharing your knowledge and techniques, you can attract a dedicated following of aspiring creators who are eager to learn from your experience. Here's a comprehensive guide on how to offer video editing tutorials and capitalize on this opportunity:

1.   Choose your niche: Determine the specific area of video editing in which you excel and where you can provide

valuable insights. It could be editing techniques for vlogs, gaming videos, travel footage, or any other niche that aligns with your expertise and interests

2.   Plan your tutorial content: Outline the topics and concepts you want to cover in your tutorials. Start with the basics and gradually progress to more advanced editing techniques. Consider breaking down complex processes into manageable steps to ensure that beginners can follow along

3.   Create high-quality tutorials: Invest in good recording and editing equipment to produce visually appealing and professional-looking tutorials. Clear audio, crisp visuals, and well-structured content enhance the learning experience for your viewers

4.   Demonstrate editing software: Choose a popular editing software and demonstrate how to navigate its features and tools. Provide step-by-step instructions, shortcuts, and practical tips to help viewers become proficient in using the software

5.   Showcase real-life examples: Incorporate real-life examples by editing footage from your videos or using stock footage. This allows viewers to see the practical application of the techniques you're teaching and better understand how they can be implemented in their projects

6.   Engage with your audience: Encourage viewers to ask questions and provide feedback in the comments section. Respond promptly to their queries, offer clarifications, and engage in discussions. This fosters a sense of community and establishes you as an authority in the field

7.   Collaborate with other creators: Collaborate with other content creators or experts in video editing to bring

fresh perspectives and insights to your tutorials. Guest appearances or interviews can add value and attract a wider audience

8. Monetize your tutorials: There are several ways to monetize your video editing tutorials. You can include advertisements in your videos and earn revenue through ad impressions or clicks. Additionally, you can promote affiliate products or services related to video editing software, equipment, or online courses and earn commissions from sales generated through your referral links

9. Offer premium content or courses: Consider offering premium content or comprehensive video editing courses for a fee. This can include in-depth tutorials, personalized feedback on viewers' editing projects, or access to exclusive resources. Providing additional value through premium offerings allows you to monetize your expertise further

10. Promote your tutorials: Utilize various marketing channels to promote your tutorials and reach a wider audience. Share your tutorials on your YouTube channel, social media platforms, relevant online communities, and even your website or blog. Collaborate with other creators or industry influencers to cross-promote each other's content

11. Stay updated: Video editing techniques and software evolve rapidly. Stay updated with the latest trends, software updates, and editing techniques to ensure that your tutorials remain relevant and valuable. Attend industry conferences, participate in online forums, and engage with the editing community to stay informed

Remember, the success of your video editing tutorials

relies on delivering high-quality content consistently. Strive for clarity, thoroughness, and engaging delivery to keep your viewers interested and coming back for more. Continuously improve your teaching skills, seek feedback from your audience, and adapt your content based on their needs and preferences.

Offering video editing tutorials not only establishes you as an authority in the field but also allows you to contribute to the growth and development of aspiring creators. By sharing your expertise, you empower others to create impactful and visually appealing content. Embrace this opportunity to educate, inspire, and monetize your passion for video editing while fostering a community of like-minded individuals.

CHAPTER EIGHTEEN

Create Sponsored Content for Patreon or Ko-fi: Work with Patreon or Ko-fi to create sponsored content that introduces their platforms to your audience.

Patreon and Ko-fi are popular platforms that enable creators to receive direct financial support from their fans and followers. As a content creator, you can leverage your influence and collaborate with Patreon or Ko-fi to create sponsored content that introduces their platforms to your audience while providing them with valuable insights on how to support creators.

Sponsored content involves partnering with a company or platform to promote its products or services to your audience in exchange for compensation. By working with Patreon or Ko-fi, you can not only generate additional income but also provide your viewers with a practical and effective way to support their favorite creators.

Here's a comprehensive guide on how to create

sponsored content for Patreon or Ko-fi:

1.   Understand the platforms: Familiarize yourself with Patreon and Ko-fi, their features, and the benefits they offer to creators. Explore their websites, read through their documentation, and engage with other creators who have experience using these platforms. This will help you grasp the nuances and intricacies of each platform, enabling you to create informed and authentic sponsored content

2.   Align with your audience: Ensure that Patreon or Ko-fi aligns with the interests and needs of your audience. Assess whether your viewers would appreciate and benefit from supporting creators through these platforms. Consider factors such as the demographics, interests, and engagement level of your audience to determine the compatibility of Patreon or Ko-fi sponsorship with your content

3.   Craft a sponsorship proposal: Develop a compelling sponsorship proposal that outlines the value you can offer to Patreon or Ko-fi and how you plan to promote their platforms. Highlight your reach, engagement metrics, and the unique perspective you bring as a content creator. Emphasize how your audience can benefit from supporting creators through these platforms and showcase any previous successful sponsorships you've had

4.   Negotiate sponsorship terms: Once you've established contact with Patreon or Ko-fi, negotiate the terms of the sponsorship. Discuss compensation, deliverables, and the duration of the sponsorship. Be open to finding a mutually beneficial arrangement that aligns with your goals, values, and audience's expectations

5.   Create engaging sponsored content: Design sponsored content that educates and excites your audience about Patreon or Ko-fi. Consider various formats such as

dedicated videos, vlogs, or blog posts that provide a comprehensive overview of the platforms, their benefits, and how they enable creators to receive direct support. Incorporate personal experiences and success stories to add authenticity and credibility to your content

6. Showcase the features: Demonstrate the key features and functionalities of Patreon or Ko-fi that make them unique and valuable to both creators and supporters. Explain how creators can offer exclusive content, rewards, or early access to their supporters through these platforms. Highlight the convenience and direct impact of supporting creators through Patreon or Ko-fi

7. Educate on the process: Walk your audience through the process of supporting creators on Patreon or Ko-fi. Explain how they can set up an account, pledge their support, and interact with creators. Provide step-by-step instructions, tips, and best practices to help your viewers navigate the platforms seamlessly

8. Emphasize the benefits: Communicate the benefits of supporting creators through Patreon or Ko-fi. Highlight how their contributions directly impact the creators' ability to produce high-quality content and continue creating the content they love. Discuss the sense of community and exclusivity that supporters can experience by being part of a creator's inner circle

9. Be transparent: Maintain transparency throughout the sponsored content by clearly disclosing that it is a sponsored partnership with Patreon or Ko-fi. This fosters trust with your audience and ensures that they are aware of the nature of the collaboration. Comply with the advertising guidelines and disclosure requirements of your platform, such as including a disclosure statement in your video description or blog post

10. Monitor and evaluate the campaign: Keep track of the performance of your sponsored content by analyzing metrics such as views, engagement, and conversions. Monitor the feedback and comments from your audience to gauge their response and adjust your approach if needed. This feedback loop will help you refine your sponsored content strategies and improve your overall content creation

11. Long-term collaborations: Consider establishing a long-term partnership with Patreon or Ko-fi to create ongoing sponsored content. This can involve periodic updates, features on successful creators using the platforms, or highlighting new features and initiatives. Building a lasting relationship with these platforms can result in continuous sponsorship opportunities and increased revenue potential

Remember, when creating sponsored content for Patreon or Ko-fi, it is crucial to maintain authenticity, and transparency, and provide genuine value to your audience. By effectively promoting these platforms, you empower your viewers to directly support their favorite creators while fostering a sense of community and collaboration within your content ecosystem.

CHAPTER NINETEEN

Develop a Mobile App or Game: Partner with developers to create a mobile app or game related to your channel's content and earn revenue through in-app purchases or ads.

In today's digital age, mobile apps and games have become a significant part of people's lives. As a content creator, you have a unique opportunity to expand your presence and monetize your brand by developing a mobile app or game that complements your channel's content. This guide will walk you through the process of creating a mobile app or game and leveraging it to generate revenue.

1. Define your concept: Start by brainstorming ideas that align with your channel's content and resonate with your audience. Consider the interests, preferences, and demographics of your viewers. Think about how your app or game can offer value, entertainment, or utility to your audience. Whether it's a fitness tracking app, a puzzle game, or a recipe organizer, ensure that it connects with your niche

and reflects your unique style

2.   Research app development options: Determine whether you want to learn app development yourself or partner with professional developers. If you choose to collaborate with developers, conduct thorough research to find reputable companies or freelancers with experience in creating mobile apps or games. Review their portfolios, client testimonials, and pricing models to identify the best fit for your project

3.   Plan your app/game features: Outline the core features and functionalities of your app or game. Consider how it can enhance user engagement, provide value, and encourage frequent usage. Design a user-friendly interface and ensure that the app/game aligns with the branding and visual style of your channel. Focus on creating a seamless and enjoyable user experience

4.   Monetization strategies: Explore various monetization strategies for your app or game. Two common methods are in-app purchases and advertising. In-app purchases allow users to buy additional features, premium content, or virtual goods within the app. Advertising involves displaying ads within the app/game and earning revenue based on impressions or clicks. Assess which method or combination thereof aligns best with your target audience and app/game concept

5.   Collaborate with developers: If you decide to partner with developers, communicate your vision, features, and monetization strategies to them. Collaborate closely throughout the development process to ensure that your app/game meets your expectations. Provide feedback, review prototypes, and suggest improvements to create a product that aligns with your brand and resonates with your audience

6. Beta testing and feedback: Conduct extensive beta testing to identify and fix any bugs, glitches, or usability issues. Invite a select group of your audience or external testers to provide feedback on the app/game's functionality, user experience, and overall appeal. Use their insights to make necessary improvements before launching the final version

7. App Store Optimization (ASO): Once your app or game is ready, focus on app store optimization to improve its visibility and discoverability. Research relevant keywords, write compelling descriptions, and design eye-catching screenshots and app icons. Optimizing these elements will increase the chances of your app/game being found by potential users in the app stores

8. Launch and promotion: Launch your app or game with a well-planned marketing campaign. Utilize your existing channel and social media platforms to create excitement and generate buzz. Publish engaging content, teasers, and trailers to pique the interest of your audience. Consider collaborating with other influencers or running targeted advertising campaigns to reach a wider audience

9. App/Game updates and community engagement: Continuously update your app or game to improve its functionality, add new features, and address user feedback. Engage with your user base by responding to reviews, addressing concerns, and incorporating their suggestions. Building a vibrant and loyal community around your app/game fosters long-term engagement and increases the chances of success

10. Analyze and optimize: Monitor the performance of your app or game using analytics tools. Track metrics such as downloads, user retention, in-app purchases, and ad

revenue. Analyze this data to identify patterns, understand user behavior, and optimize your monetization strategies. Experiment with different approaches to find the most effective ways to generate revenue

Creating a mobile app or game related to your channel's content provides a new avenue for monetization and audience engagement. By partnering with developers and offering an immersive and interactive experience, you can expand your brand presence, attract new audiences, and generate revenue through in-app purchases and advertising. Embrace the opportunities offered by the mobile app and gaming industry to further establish yourself as a content creator and provide value to your viewers.

CHAPTER TWENTY

Public Speaking Engagements: Establish yourself as an expert in your niche and secure speaking engagements or workshops at conferences or events.

Public speaking engagements can be a powerful way to expand your influence, showcase your expertise, and generate revenue as a content creator. By establishing yourself as an expert in your niche and securing speaking opportunities at conferences, events, or workshops, you can not only connect with your audience on a deeper level but also open doors to new opportunities. This guide will provide you with a comprehensive overview of how to leverage public speaking engagements to enhance your brand and monetize your expertise.

1. Identify your niche and expertise: Begin by identifying your niche and the specific area in which you have expertise. Consider your channel's content and the topics that resonate most with your audience. Determine what sets you apart and makes you uniquely qualified to

speak on those subjects. This will help you position yourself as an authority and attract speaking opportunities

2.   Build your speaking portfolio: Start building your speaking portfolio by seeking opportunities to speak at local events, meetups, or workshops. Offer to share your knowledge and insights with relevant communities, educational institutions, or industry associations. These early speaking engagements will provide valuable experience, allow you to refine your presentation skills, and help you gather testimonials and references for future opportunities

3.   Develop compelling speaking topics: Craft a list of compelling speaking topics that align with your niche and cater to the interests of your target audience. Choose subjects that are relevant, timely, and offer practical value. Focus on delivering actionable insights, thought-provoking ideas, or inspiring stories that leave a lasting impact on your audience

4.   Create a speaker reel and media kit: Assemble a professional speaker reel and media kit that showcases your speaking engagements, highlights your expertise, and provides an overview of your content and audience demographics. Include testimonials, past speaking engagements, notable achievements, and media coverage to build credibility and attract event organizers

5.   Research and target relevant events: Research conferences, industry events, or workshops that align with your niche. Look for events where your target audience is likely to attend and where your expertise will be valued. Take note of submission deadlines, speaking tracks, and any specific requirements for speaker applications

6.   Craft compelling proposals: Tailor your speaking

proposals to each event or conference you target. Clearly articulate the value you bring, the key takeaways from your presentation, and how your session aligns with the event's theme or objectives. Emphasize the unique perspective you bring as a content creator and the benefits attendees will gain from hearing you speak

7.   Leverage your network: Tap into your network to discover speaking opportunities. Reach out to industry contacts, fellow content creators, or event organizers to express your interest in speaking at their events or to seek recommendations for relevant conferences. Building relationships and collaborations within your niche can lead to valuable speaking engagements

8.   Engage with event organizers: Once you've identified potential speaking opportunities, engage with event organizers through email, social media, or networking events. Introduce yourself, express your interest in speaking, and provide a brief overview of your expertise and topics. Be professional, and persistent, and showcase your enthusiasm to capture the attention of event organizers

9.   Deliver impactful presentations: Prepare diligently for your speaking engagements by creating engaging and well-structured presentations. Tailor your content to the specific audience and event, ensuring it is informative, entertaining, and memorable. Incorporate multimedia elements, storytelling techniques, and interactive components to keep your audience engaged throughout your presentation

10. Promote your speaking engagements: Once you secure speaking engagements, actively promote them to your audience and social media followers. Create dedicated content, such as announcement videos, blog posts, or social media updates, to build anticipation and encourage

attendance. Leverage your existing platforms to spread the word and generate buzz around your speaking opportunities

11. Monetize your speaking engagements: There are several ways to monetize your speaking engagements. You can negotiate speaker fees with event organizers, especially for larger conferences or corporate events. Additionally, you can offer additional services such as workshops, consulting sessions, or coaching packages to attendees who are interested in further engaging with your expertise

12. Expand your speaking opportunities: As you gain experience and establish your credibility as a speaker, actively seek out larger conferences, international events, or high-profile speaking engagements. Consider joining speaker bureaus or talent agencies that can help connect you with premium speaking opportunities and negotiate speaking fees on your behalf

13. Continuously refine your speaking skills: Regularly evaluate and refine your speaking skills by seeking feedback from event organizers, audience members, and peers. Attend speaking workshops or join Toastmasters clubs to further develop your presentation abilities, stage presence, and delivery techniques

Public speaking engagements provide a platform to showcase your expertise, connect with your audience on a personal level, and monetize your knowledge as a content creator. By establishing yourself as an expert, targeting relevant events, delivering impactful presentations, and effectively promoting your speaking opportunities, you can not only generate revenue but also expand your reach and influence within your niche. Embrace the power of public speaking and unlock the potential to elevate your brand and career as a content creator.

ABOUT THE AUTHOR

The author is a seasoned finance, accounting, and tax professional with over four decades of experience in different industries. He has great interest for teaching, blogging and digital marketing and he helps individuals develop their skills and excel in their respective careers.

Printed in Great Britain
by Amazon